Far East My Chinese Book

远东儿童中文

Simplified Character

Workbook
作业本

Wei-ling Wu（吴威玲）
Yuti Chao（赵玉娣）
Shin-Yin Estes（萧欣音）
Chai-Ho Lo（胡采禾）

The Far East Book Co., Ltd.

Published by
The Far East Book Co., Ltd.
66-1 Chungking South Road, Section 1
Taipei, Taiwan
www.fareast.com.tw

远东图书公司出版印行 版权所有 翻印必究
©2008 The Far East Book Co., Ltd.
All rights reserved. No part of this publication may be reproduced or transmitted in any form or by any means, electronic or mechanical, including photocopy, recording, or any information storage or retrieval system, without permission in writing from the publisher.

North America Distributor
Elite Culture Educational Co.
www.eliteculture.com

ISBN 978-957-612-711-3

Acknowledgements

My Chinese Book is the result of the combined efforts of many people over the past eight years.

In 1996, under the leadership of its former Executive Director, Scott McVay, the Geraldine R. Dodge Foundation, launched the Chinese Initiative for Children. This effort, assisted by the Secondary School Chinese Language Center at Princeton University, extended the Foundation's support for Chinese language instruction to elementary schools. Five years ago, David Grant, the present Executive Director of the Dodge Foundation committed continuous support to the Initiative. The contributions from the Dodge Foundation have made the Chinese Initiative for Children one of the most important developments in elementary education in recent years.

Many principals have also been playing a crucial role in program implementation. The New Jersey elementary schools that have participated in Chinese Initiative for Children since 1997 are: Avon Elementary School (Principal: *Anthony Arcodia*); Bartle School (former Principal: *Collette Breen*, present Principal: *Andrea Orlando*); Clinton School (former Principal: *Hazel Davis*, present Principal: *William Rhinehart*); Evergreen Ave. School (Principal: *Frances Carey*); Forest Avenue School (Principal: *Debra Pavignano*); Horace Mann Elementary School (Principal: *Robert Sweeney*); Irving Primary School (former Principal: *Andrew Mignano*, present Principal: *Matthew Barbosa*); Kingston School (Principal: *Stanley W. Sheckman*); Lawnside School District (Principal: *Joyce C. Payne*); Princeton Friends School (Principal: *Jane Fremon*); Thomas Paine Elementary School (former Principal: *Max Wald*, present Principal: *Lawyer Chapman*); Tuscan Elementary School (Principal: *Arlene Pincus*); Wicoff School (former Principal: *Denise Mengani*, present Principal: *Brian Stevens*); Woodland School (Principal: *Patricia Moore*); and Upper Elementary School (Principal: *Kevin Brennan*).

The Teacher Group, which is supported by the Geraldine R. Dodge Foundation, has given teachers the opportunity to work as a cooperative team to create instructional materials along with the program development. In the past eight years, the following teachers have contributed to the initial work on textbooks: *Vicky Chang, Shin-Yin Estes, Yuti Chao, Heping Jiang, Jing-lan Ku, Ning-Shing Kung, Yi Chia Lee, Ruohmin Maria Liao, Shu-jen Liu, Chai-Ho Lo, Kuo-Tsai Chang Pan, Jume Shen, Ming Yeh, Guoping Wan, and Wei-ling Wu* (coordinator of the Teacher Group).

Since the fall of 2000, *Shin-Yin Estes, Yuti Chao, Chai-Ho Lo* and *Wei-ling Wu* have been working together, revising and finalizing *My Chinese Book* for publication.

Last but not the least, our sincere thanks go to John Pu, Peter Pu, Xuefang Lin and staff members of the Far East Book Company in Taiwan for their enthusiasm and efforts in making *My Chinese Book* an enjoyable experience for American children.

The Authors

Contents

Sheet 1-1	p.1
Sheet 1-2	p.3
Sheet 1-3	p.5
Sheet 2-1	p.7
Sheet 2-2	p.9
Sheet 2-3	p.11
Sheet 3-1	p.13
Sheet 3-2	p.15
Sheet 3-3	p.17
Sheet 4-1	p.19
Sheet 4-2	p.21
Sheet 4-3	p.23
Sheet 5-1	p.25
Sheet 5-2	p.27
Sheet 5-3	p.29
Sheet 6-1	p.31
Sheet 6-2	p.33
Sheet 6-3	p.35
Sheet 7-1	p.37
Sheet 7-2	p.39
Sheet 7-3	p.41
Sheet 8-1	p.43
Sheet 8-2	p.45
Sheet 8-3	p.47

My Chinese Book ② Workbook
儿童中文②作业本

Name: _____

Sheet 1-1

Listen, Say and Color:

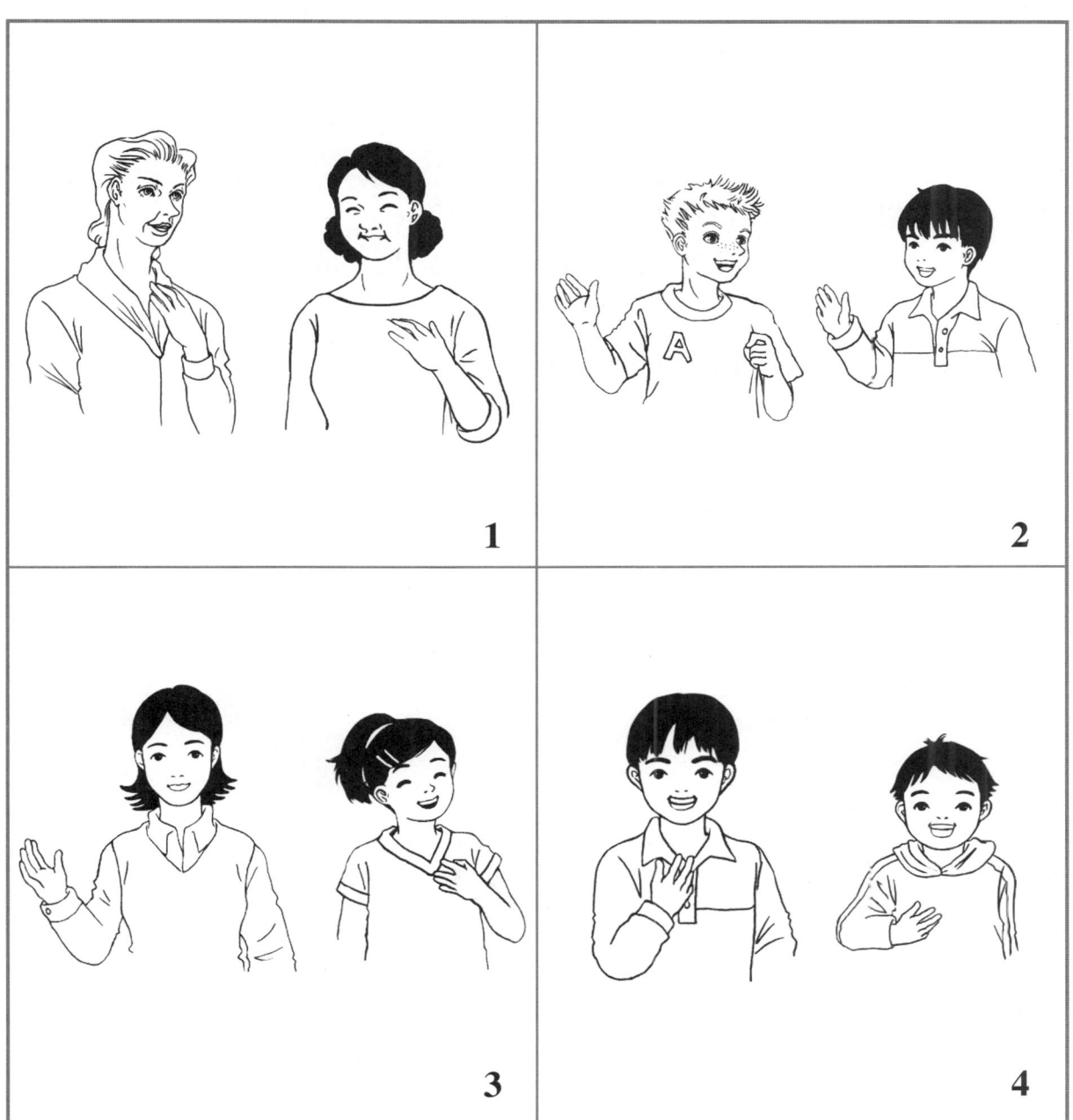

Directions:

Teacher : Yī hào. Wǒ shì Měiguó rén.
Children: Wǒ shì Měiguó rén. (Color the American person.)

Teacher : Èr hào. Wǒ shì Zhōngguó rén.
Children: Wǒ shì Zhōngguó rén. (Color the Chinese person.)

Teacher : Sān hào. Wǒ shì lǎoshī.
Children: Wǒ shì lǎoshī. (Color the teacher.)

Teacher : Sì hào. Wǒ shì dìdi.
Children: Wǒ shì dìdi. (Color the younger brother.)

Sheet 1-2

Listen, Say and Color:

Directions:

Teacher : Yī hào. Měiguó rén.

Children: Měiguó rén. (Color the American person.)

Teacher : Èr hào. Zhōngguó rén.

Children: Zhōngguó rén. (Color the Chinese person.)

Teacher : Sān hào. Yīngwén.

Children: Yīngwén. (Color the word "English.")

Teacher : Sì hào. Zhōngwén.

Children: Zhōngwén. (Color the characters "中文.")

My Chinese Book ② Workbook
儿童中文②作业本

Name:

Sheet 1-3

Listen, Say and Connect:

Directions:

Teacher : Bàba xué Yīngwén.

Children: Bàba xué Yīngwén. (Connect the father with the English textbook as indicated in the worksheet.)

Repeat with the rest people in the same manner.
Also, the teacher can give directions using different verbs such as kàn, tīng, shuō.

My Chinese Book ② Workbook
儿童中文②作业本

Name:

Sheet 2-1

Listen and Mark the China Days on the Calendar:

Week 1

Sunday	Monday	Tuesday	Wednesday	Thursday	Friday	Saturday

Week 2

Sunday	Monday	Tuesday	Wednesday	Thursday	Friday	Saturday

Week 3

Sunday	Monday	Tuesday	Wednesday	Thursday	Friday	Saturday

Week 4

Sunday	Monday	Tuesday	Wednesday	Thursday	Friday	Saturday

Directions:

Teacher : Our school will have a China Day in each week. Listen and mark these days on the calendar. Week One, xīngqī sān.

Children: Xīngqī sān. (Children may draw a pair of chopsticks, a lantern, or a panda to indicate the China Day.)

Repeat with the other three weeks.

Sheet 2-2

Talk about Plans for Tomorrow:

Directions:

Teacher : Jīntiān xīngqī jǐ?

Children: Xīngqī wǔ.

Teacher : Míngtiān xīngqī jǐ?

Children: Xīngqī liù.

Teacher : Hǎo jí le! Míngtiān xīngqī liù. Bàba qù dǎqiú.

Children: Bàba qù dǎqiú. (Connect the father with the picture of playing basketball as indicated in the worksheet.)

Repeat with the other family members.

My Chinese Book ② Workbook
儿童中文②作业本

Name:

Sheet 2-3

Make Plans:

Directions:

Option 1—Use this worksheet as a listen-and-connect activity.

    Teacher : Xīngqī wǔ, xué Yīngwén.

    Children : Xīngqī wǔ, xué Yīngwén. (Connect Friday with the picture of learning English as indicated in the worksheet.)

Repeat with the other days in a random order.

Option 2—Use this worksheet as a self-decision-making sheet.
Children connect the days of the week with action pictures at their own choice. Then the teacher displays children's plans on the wall and talks about them. Or, children present their plans one by one to the class. Other children comment on the plans by saying, "Hǎo jí le!"

My Chinese Book ② Workbook
儿童中文②作业本

Name:

Sheet 3-1

Listen, Say and Circle:

13

Directions:

Teacher : Yī hào. Rè.

Children: Rè. (Circle the pot on the stove.)

Repeat with the other three pictures by saying, "Rè," or "Lěng."

Sheet 3-2

Listen, Say and Connect:

Sunday

Monday

Tuesday

Wednesday

Thursday

Friday

Saturday
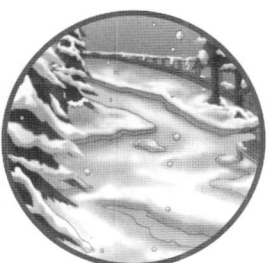

Directions:

Teacher : Xīngqī tiān, xiàyǔ.

Children: Xīngqī tiān, xiàyǔ. (Connect Sunday with the picture of a rainy day as indicated in the worksheet.)

Repeat with the rest of the days.

My Chinese Book ② Workbook
儿童中文②作业本

Name:

Sheet 3-3

Create Weather Conditions for This Unbelievable Week:

Directions:

Ask children to draw weather conditions for each box. Invite some children to present their creation to the class. Or, the teacher shows some children's drawings to the class and asks questions about the weather conditions.

Sheet 4-1

Listen, Say and Write Down the Numbers:

Directions:

Teacher : Yī hào, yáng.

Children: Yáng. (Write the number "1" on the sheep body as indicated in the worksheet.)

Repeat with the other six animals: gǒu, māo, jī, zhū, niú, yā.

My Chinese Book ② Workbook
儿童中文②作业本

Name:

Sheet 4-2

Listen and Color:

Directions:

Teacher : Zhū shì hóngsè de.

Children: (Find the pig and color it red.)

Repeat with the other six animals: gǒu, māo, jī, yáng, niú, yā.

Name:

Sheet 4-3

What Animals Do They Like?

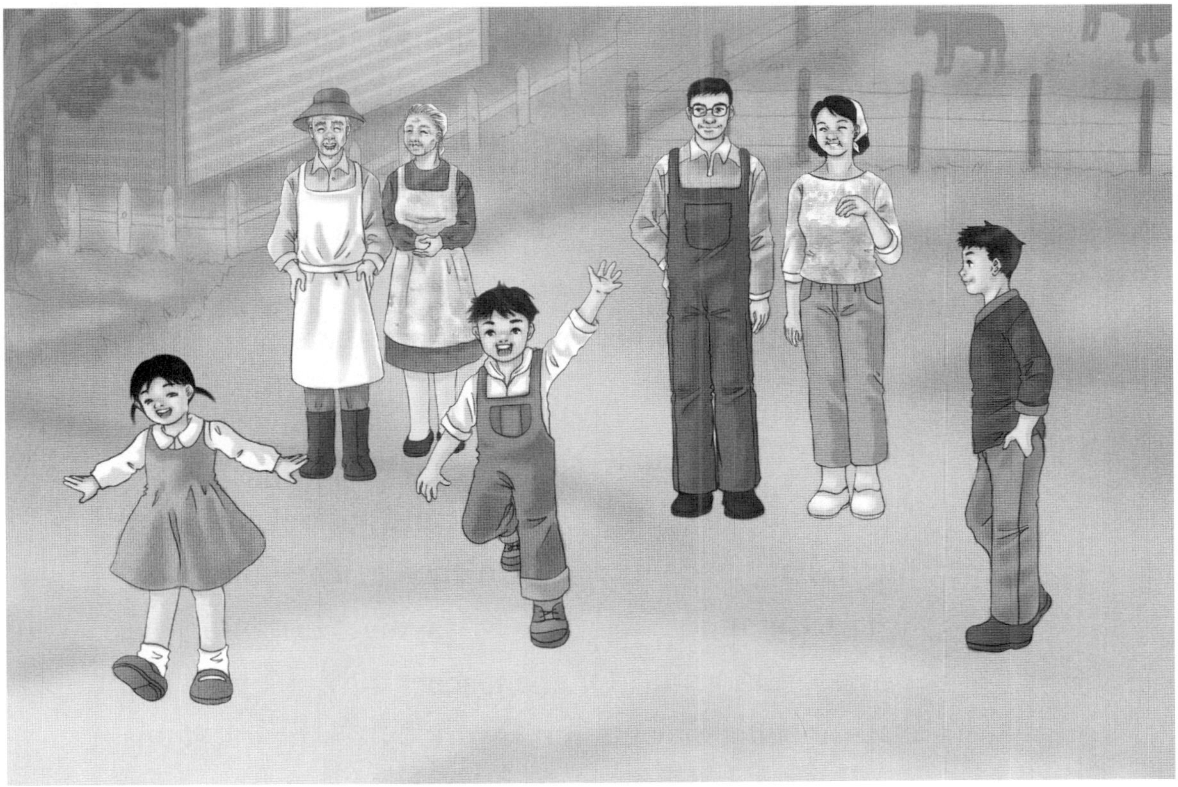

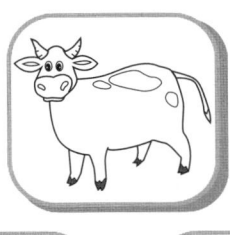

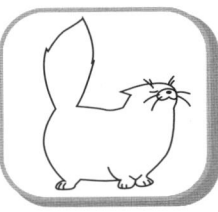

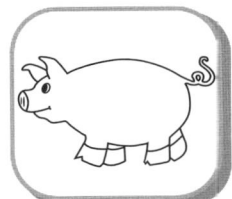

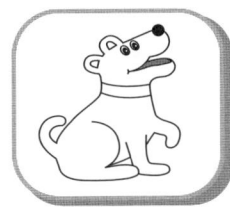

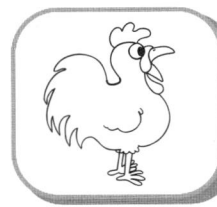

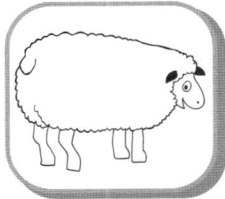

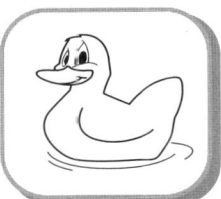

Directions:

Option 1—Use this worksheet as a listening comprehension activity.

        Teacher : Yéye xǐhuān niú.

        Children : (Find the cow. Cut it and paste beside the grandfather.)

        Repeat with the other six family members.

Option 2—Use this worksheet as a self-decision-making sheet. Children color the animals. Cut and paste them beside family members at their own choice. Then they take turns to present to the class by saying, "Zhè shì yéye. Yéye xǐhuān niú." Or, the teacher may talk with the class about some children's work by asking questions such as: Zhè shì shéi? Zhè shì shénme? Yéye xǐhuān shénme? Xiǎo niú zěnme jiào? Xiǎo niú shì shénme yánsè de?

Sheet 5-1

Listen, Say and Color:

Directions:

Teacher : Zhū shì hóngsè de.

Children: Zhū shì hóngsè de. (Find the pig and color it red.)

Repeat with the other eleven animals by using different colors for them.

Sheet 5-2

Cut and Paste:

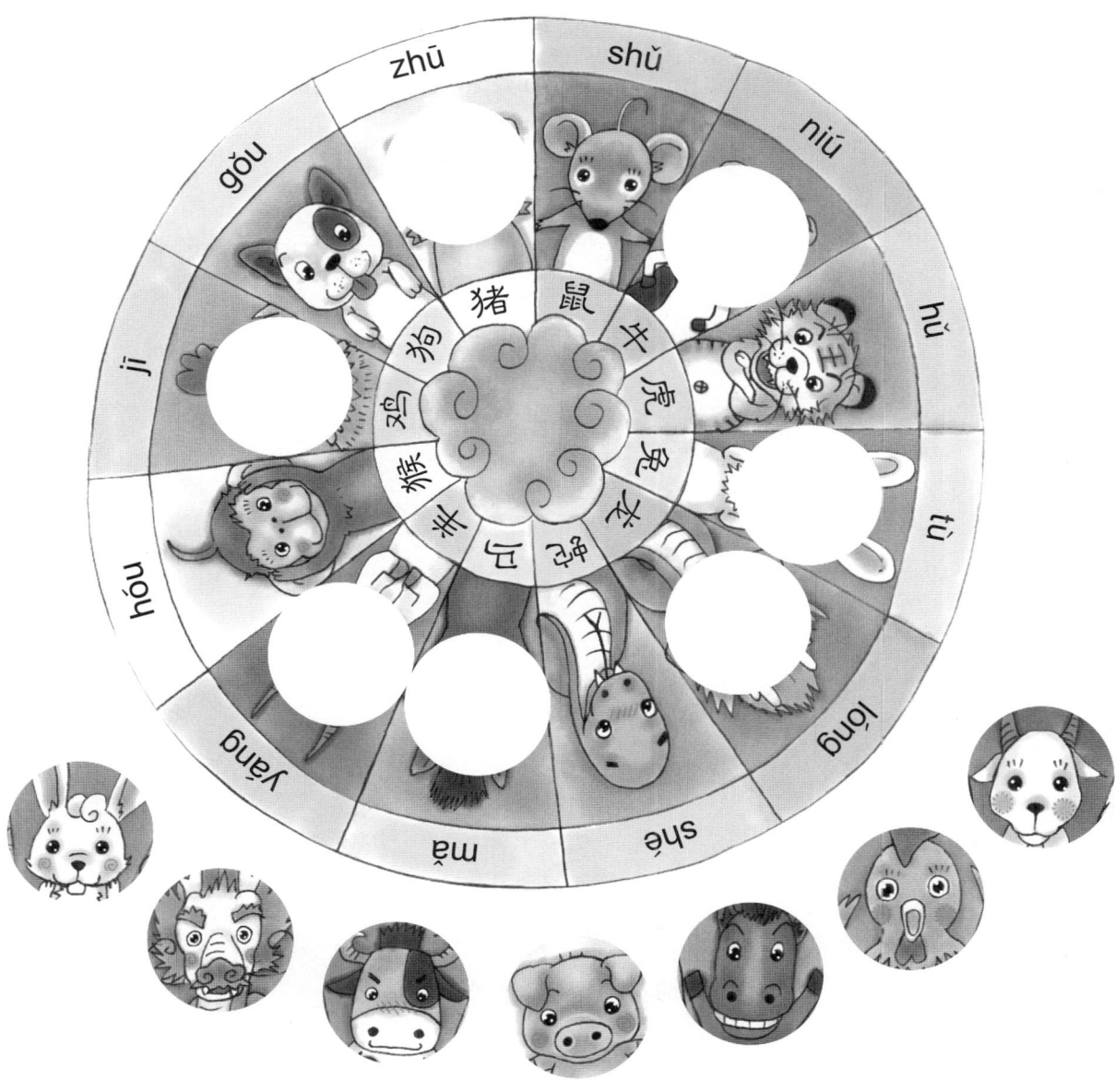

Directions:

Teacher : Cut the animals at the bottom of the page.
Paste them in the right position in the chart.

Sheet 5-3

Find the Twelve Zodiac Animals and Color Them:

Directions:

Teacher : Find the twelve animals of the Chinese Zodiac in the picture.

Circle and color them.

My Chinese Book ② Workbook
儿童中文②作业本

Name:

Sheet 6-1

Listen and Connect:

31

Directions:

Teacher : Hóuzi xǐhuān chī xiāngjiāo.

Children: (Find the monkey and the bananas. Draw a line to connect them as shown in the worksheet.)

Repeat with the other eleven animals.

My Chinese Book ② Workbook
儿童中文②作业本

Name:

Sheet 6-2

Listen and Draw:

Directions:

Teacher : Zhōngguó yéye yào xīguā.

Children: (Find the Chinese grandpa and draw a watermelon in his hand as shown in the worksheet.)

Repeat with the other seven people.

Sheet 6-3

Listen and Connect:

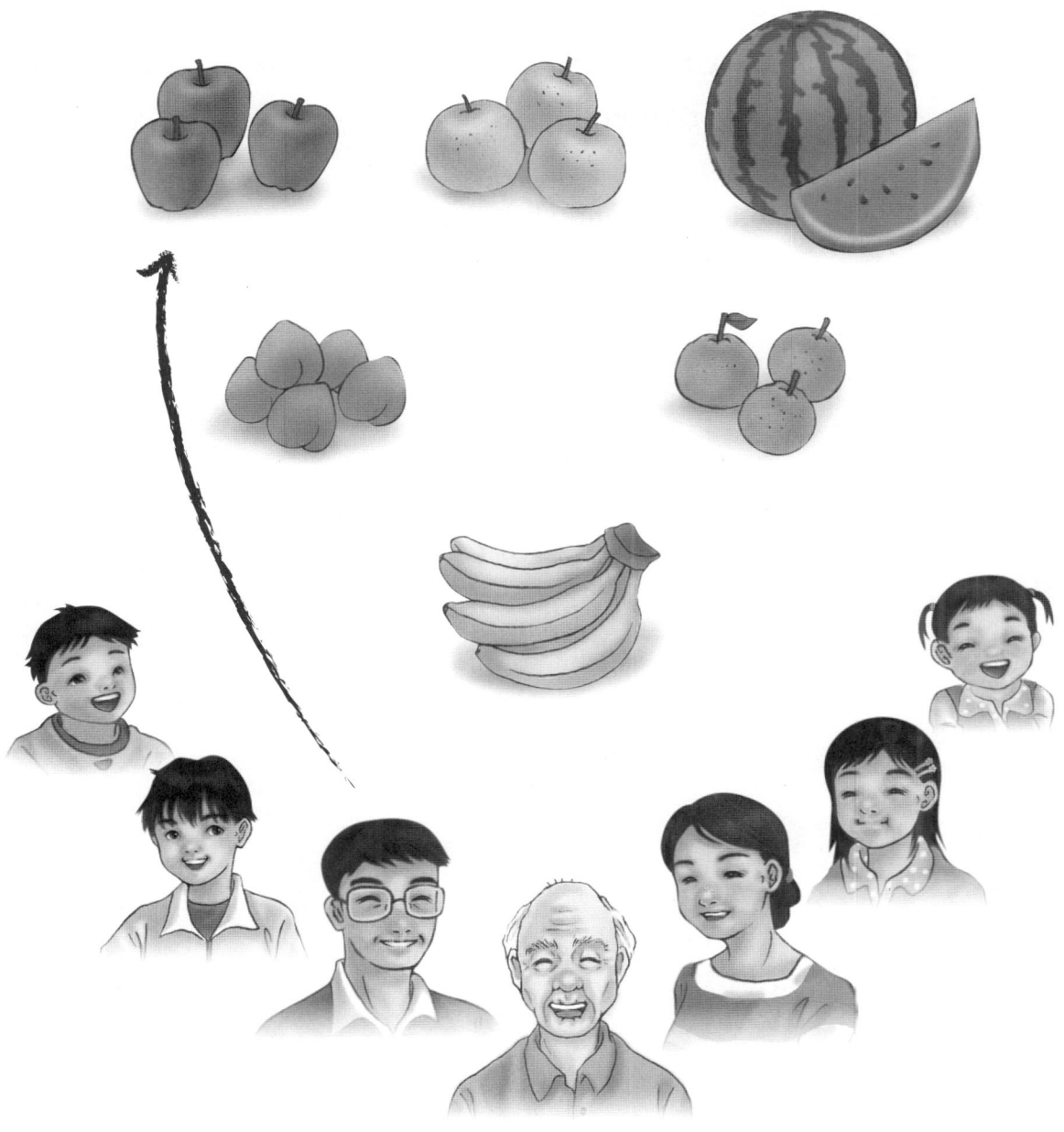

Directions:

Teacher : Bàba chī píngguǒ.

Children: (Find the father and the apples, then connect them as shown in the worksheet.)

Repeat with the other six family members.
Give directions to let two people eat watermelon.

My Chinese Book ② Workbook
儿童中文②作业本

Name:

Sheet 7-1

Listen, Say and Circle:

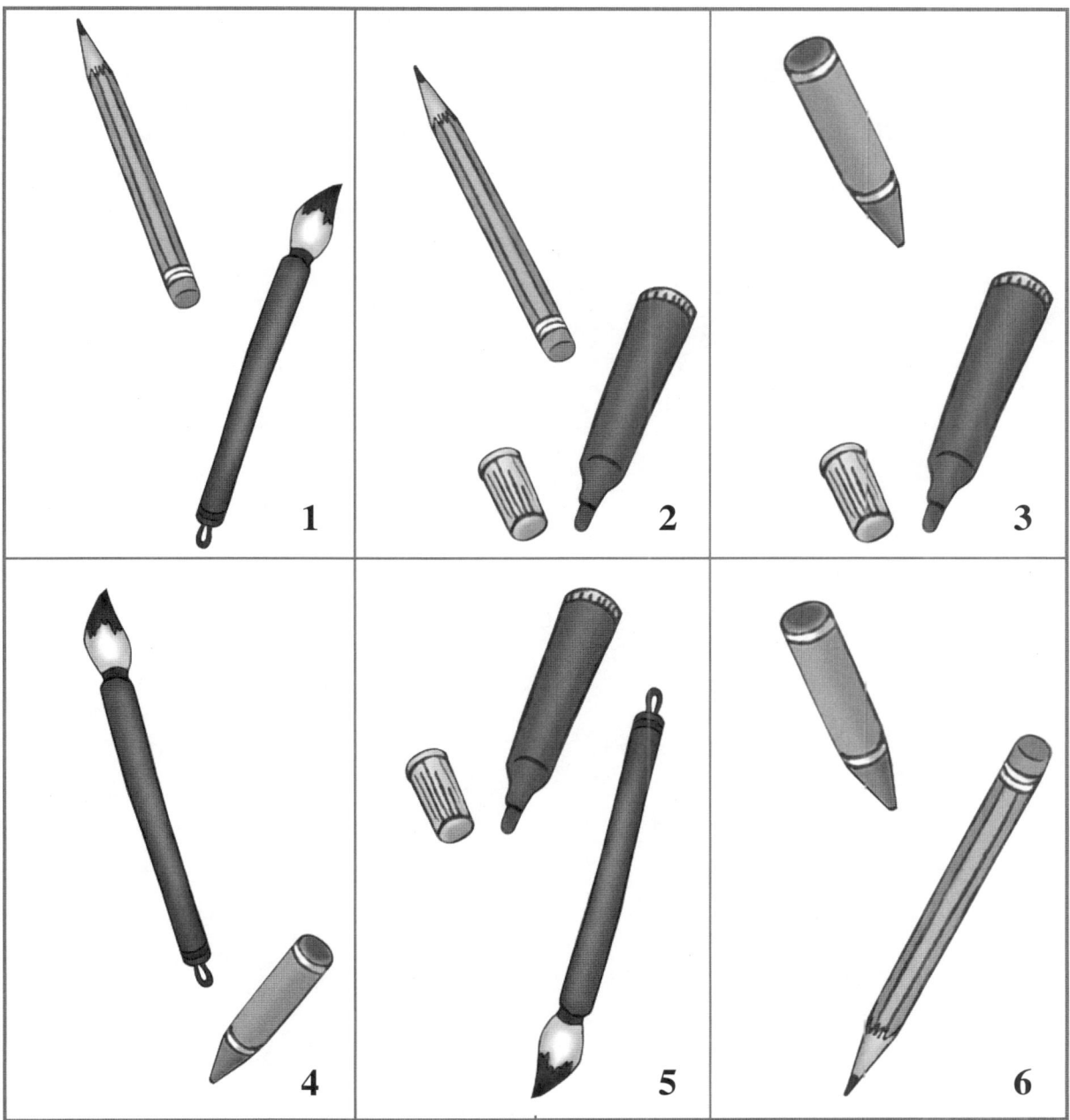

37

Directions:

Teacher : Yī hào, máobǐ.

Children : (Find the Chinese writing brush in Box 1. Say "máobǐ" and circle it.)

Repeat with the other five pictures.

Sheet 7-2

Listen and Color:

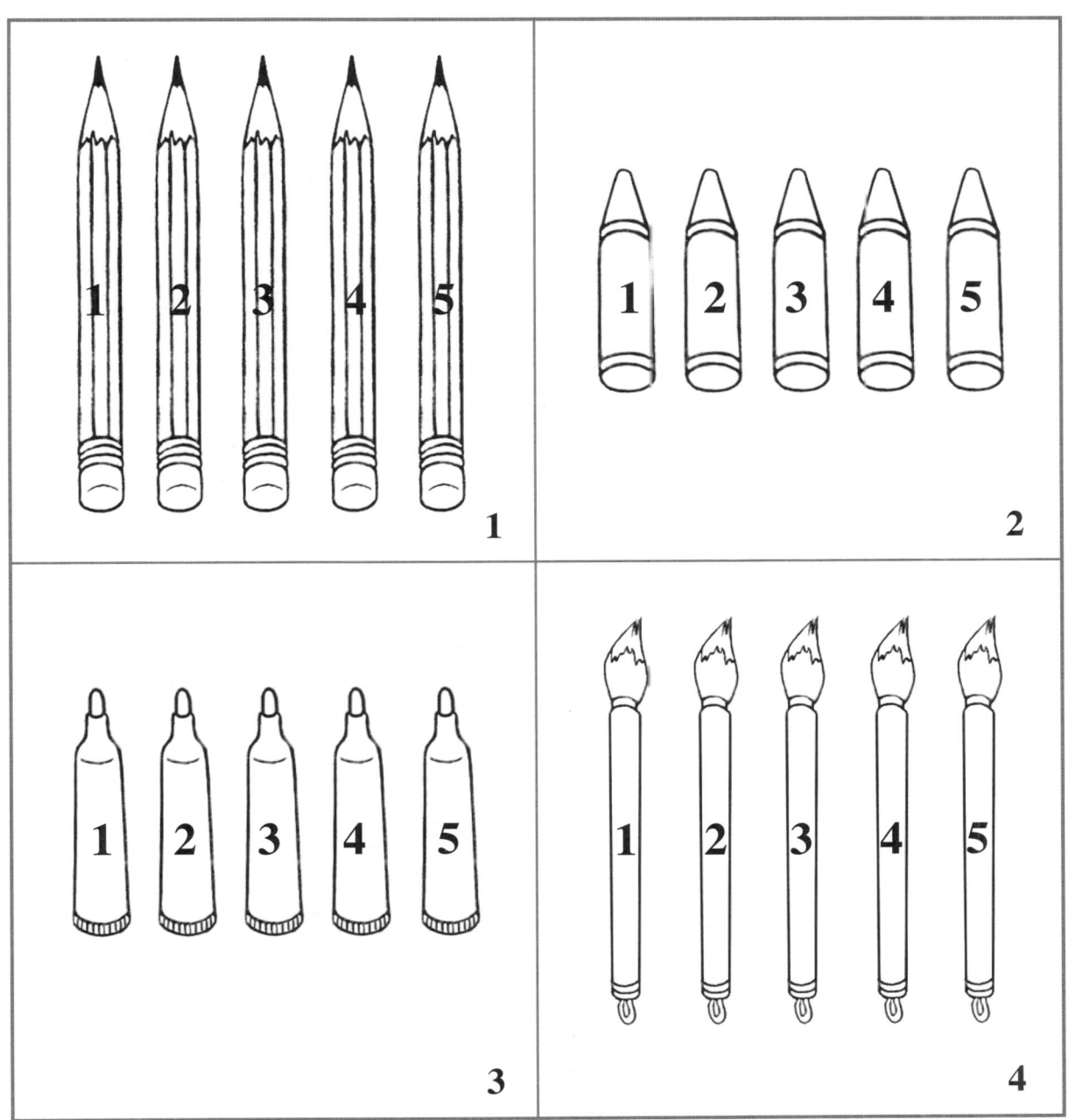

Directions:

Teacher : Qiānbǐ, sān hào, hóngsè.

Children : (Find the box for the pencils. Find Pencil #3. Color it red.)
Repeat with other pencils in Box 1.

Continue the activity with the other three boxes.

Sheet 7-3

Listen and Put Numbers in the Speech Bubbles to Make a Picture Story:

Directions:

Teacher : Yī hào, Dōngdong shuō, "**Zàijiàn!**"

Children : (Find the picture that has Dongdong saying "Good-bye." Write the number "1" in the speech bubble as indicated in the worksheet.)

Repeat with the rest pictures by saying the following for children to hear and number the speech bubbles:

Èr hào, Fāngfang shuō, "**Āiyā!**"
Sān hào, Dōngdong shuō, "**Duìbuqǐ!**"
Sì hào, Fāngfang shuō, "**Zhè shì nǐ de gǒu.**"
Wǔ hào, Míngming shuō, "**Xièxie!**"
Liù hào, Fāngfang shuō, "**Zàijiàn!**" Dōngdong shuō, "**Zàijiàn!**" Míngming shuō, "**Zàijiàn!**"

Ask children to tell the story following the numbers of the pictures.

Sheet 8-1

Listen, Say and Circle:

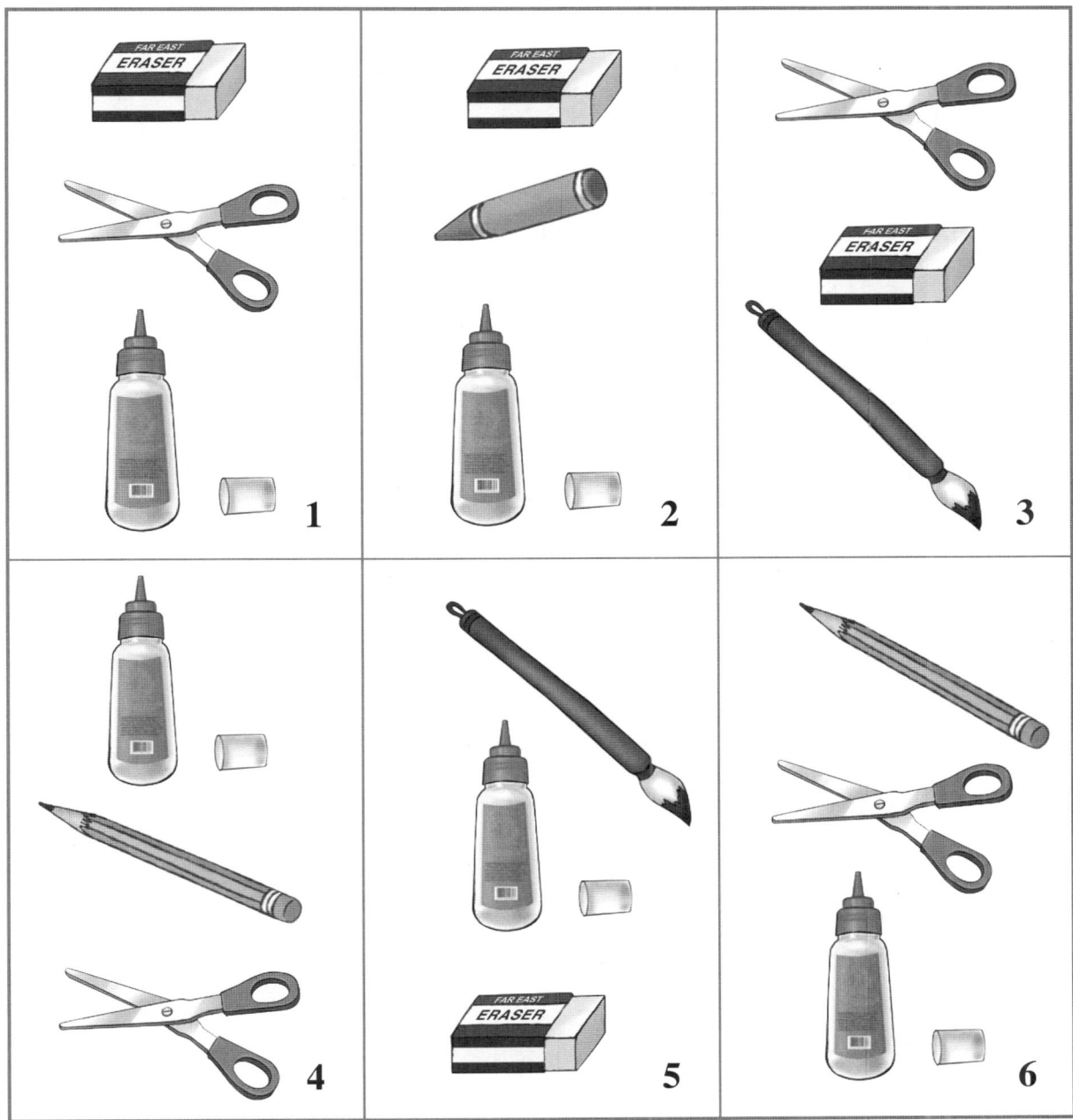

Directions:

Teacher : Yī hào, xiàngpí.

Children : (Find the eraser in Box 1. Say "xiàngpí" and circle it.)

Repeat with the other five pictures.

Sheet 8-2

Listen, Say and Color:

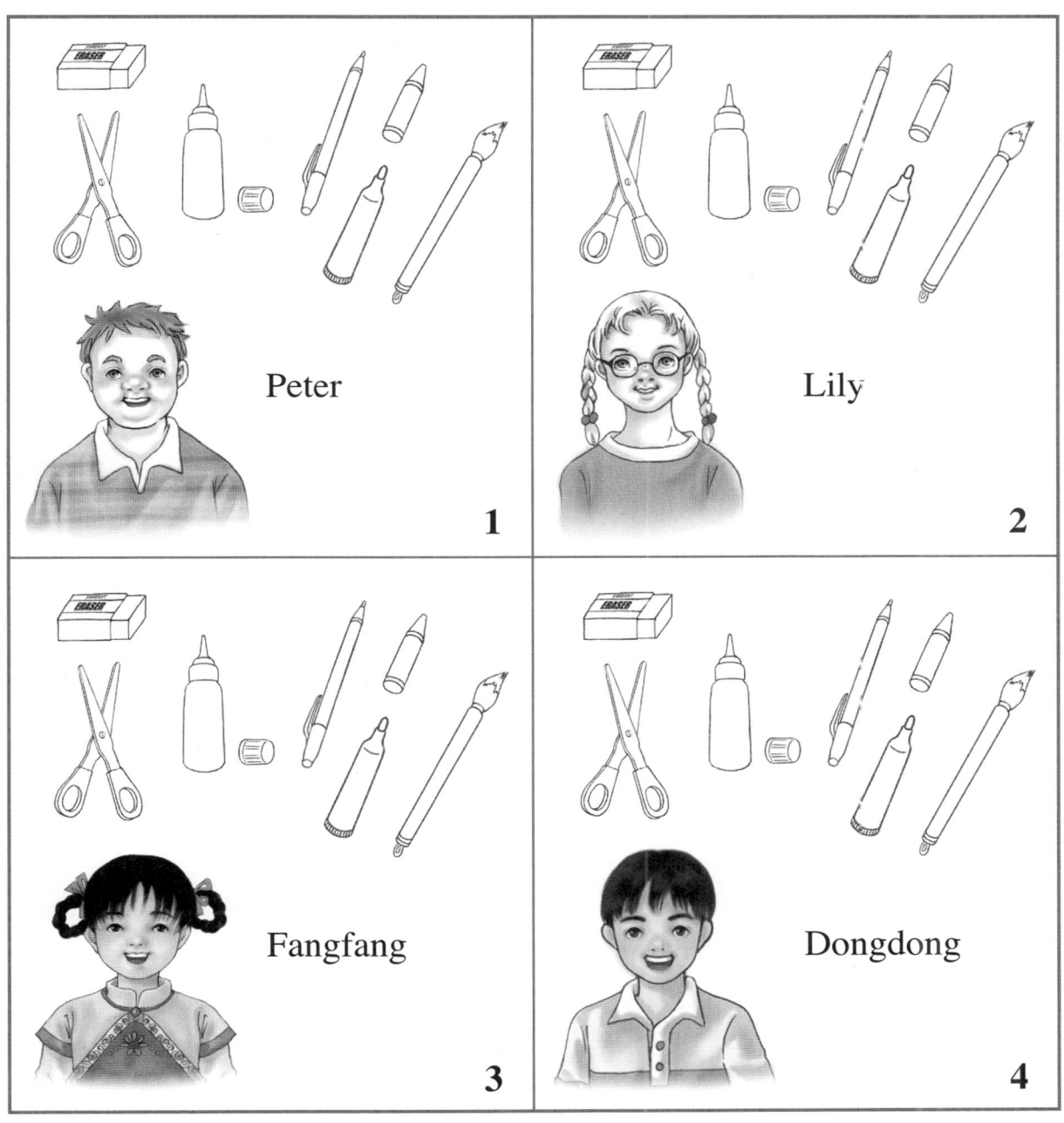

Directions:

Teacher : Peter yǒu hóng jiǎndāo.

Children : Peter yǒu hóng jiǎndāo. (Color the scissors red.)

Teacher : Peter méiyǒu xiàngpí.

Children : Peter méiyǒu xiàngpí. (Make a big ✗ over the eraser.)

Continue with a few more items in Box 1.

Repeat with the other three pictures.

My Chinese Book ② Workbook
儿童中文②作业本

Name:

Sheet 8-3

Listen, Say and Find Out:

Directions:

Teacher : (Picture 1) Peter yǒu méiyǒu......?

Children : (If yes, say, "yǒu" and put a big √ in the right box.)

(If not, say, "méiyǒu" and put a big ✗ in the right box.)

Repeat with the other five pictures:

　　　　Picture 2: Fāngfang yǒu méiyǒu......?

　　　　Picture 3: Yéye yǒu méiyǒu......?

　　　　Picture 4: Dìdi yǒu méiyǒu......?

　　　　Picture 5: Xiǎo gǒu yǒu méiyǒu......?

　　　　Picture 6: Xiǎo yā yǒu méiyǒu......?